PORTFOLIO 2

METROPOLITAN SEMINARS IN ART

Portfolio 2 · *Realism*

by John Canaday

ART EDITOR AND CRITIC
THE NEW YORK TIMES

THE METROPOLITAN MUSEUM OF ART

Printed in U.S.A.

REALISM

The Painter and the World Around Us

A PAINTING is a triple experience—visual, emotional, and intellectual. Since it is hardly possible to look at anything without reacting to it in one way or another, a certain amount of emotional response is inevitable. In character and degree this response depends on the material the painter offers us and on our willingness and capacity to respond. But when it comes to the intellectual enjoyment of painting our reaction is less immediate. It is more a matter of learning, and this is the point where the average person begins to protest his ignorance of what art is all about.

This protest is a natural defense in a time when art is subjected to so much intellectual snobbery. The layman naturally takes refuge in the conviction that all intellectualization about painting is snobbery. In its tiredest form his protest is the familiar "I don't know anything about art, but I know what I like." Translated into more formal jargon the same thing can be said this way: "Intellectual understanding of painting is not prerequisite to emotional response." Stated either way the proposition is only half true, but, all other considerations aside, it is true that intellectual appreciation of painting is a pleasure that need not involve snobbism.

This and our next two portfolios are concerned with visual, emotional, and intellectual elements in painting—seeing, feeling, and thinking. Obviously, too, when we look at a picture, what we see, what we feel, and what we think are so bound together they cannot easily be separated. But insofar as distinctions can be made we are going to consider the visual, emotional, and intellectual enjoyment of painting in individual portfolios called Realism, Expressionism, and Abstraction.

Three Violins

To begin, it would be a good idea to take the first three illustrations for this portfolio and put them side by side for comparison. Harnett's *The Old Violin* (Plate 13) is a realistic painting; Dufy's *The Yellow Violin* (Plate 14) is an expressionistic one; and Braque's *Musical Forms* (Plate 15) is an abstraction. Their subjects are as nearly parallel as one could hope for in demonstrating such divergent conceptions.

Harnett's *The Old Violin* is the kind of realistic painting the eager but unenlightened beginner encounters with relief. He knows that Harnett must be good because, after all, museums and collectors covet his work. But at the same time it is possible to enjoy Harnett without having to wonder what his art is all about. His pictures are guaranteed to be good, yet at the same time they are enjoyable at face value. In short, they are safe.

But confronted by Dufy's expressionistic painting *The Yellow Violin* our hypothetical beginner may feel a little insecure. He may find the picture attractive enough in its way, but it doesn't look as if it had been hard enough to do. Still, it is not too puzzling. You can tell what the images are supposed to represent even if they are out of kilter.

But Braque's abstraction is another matter altogether. It looks confused, pointless, inept, and even unfinished.

Yet the two paintings that are closest to one another as far as the artist's approach is concerned, the two that can be enjoyed on most nearly the same basis are the two that seem most unlike to the layman. The very realistic *Old Violin* and the highly abstract *Musical Forms* are first cousins.

Figure 1

Realism
Harnett's The Old Violin

In the original of *The Old Violin*, the objects assembled are close to life size, increasing the illusion of reality. But even in our smaller reproduction it is as if we could take the violin off its nail. We can read the score of the music and the address on the envelope (*Figure 1*). The metal ring hangs so naturally that we can imagine lifting it; the rough spots and cracks in the old door look like real imperfections in the surface of the picture instead of painted ones; the missing bolt in the hinge seems actually to have left a hole. The difference between the surface of the hinge and the portion of it formerly covered by this bolt is as credible as if truly the result of differences in exposure, fading, and rusting, instead of Harnett's skillful imitation. The whole painting amazes and fascinates by its illusionism. It is the kind of picture people want to touch, since every passage expresses a different texture so convincingly. It is hard to believe that the texture is uniformly smooth over the entire surface of the picture, as, of course, it is.

If this were the whole content of *The Old Violin* it would be a conglomeration of tricky simulations, nothing more, and would lose our interest once we had examined the imitated objects. But it continues to hold us. It holds us because it is more than an imitation of visual fact; it is a work of art. This "natural" painting is not natural at all except from detail to detail. The arrangement of the objects, for one thing, is arbitrary. As an example, it is no accident that the bow is placed vertically, lining up with other verticals such as the axis of the violin, the crack between the two boards in the background, the vertical portion of the hinges, and even the right and left borders of the picture itself, which we never think of as part of a painting although the artist is conscious that they must be incorporated into his arrangement.

The long arms of the hinges are placed on horizontal axes as precise as the verticals. They repeat the top and bottom lines of the canvas, but the bottom hinge is at a slightly greater distance from the edge of the picture than the top one is. Why? Because the hinges define a kind of secondary frame embracing the other objects, like the mats used around some pictures. A good framer makes the bottom border of a mat wider than the top and sides, since it tends to look narrower if all four are uniform.

Harnett applies this principle along with other variations not noticeable at first glance. In memory you would probably describe the violin as hanging in the center of the picture. It does not. It hangs just to one side, although it is the focal center of a nicely adjusted balance of miscellaneous objects. The sheet of music and the envelope are turned at almost forty-five degrees to the verticals and horizontals and are at almost identical angles to one another. If they were at exactly forty-five degrees or if they were not modified by curled and bent edges, the effect would be unpleasantly rigid in combination with the strict horizontals and verticals. As it is, the slight curls and bends serve as transitions to the elegant and emphatic curves played in final contrast with the straight lines—the curves of the violin's shell, the curves of its S-shaped openings, the circle of the iron ring. Imagine shifting any of these elements; imagine, for instance, eliminating the little scrap of printed paper near the violin or moving it to the other side exactly opposite the iron ring for more obvious balance, and you will see how carefully every object has been disposed and how arbitrarily.

That is the point. Ultimately this naturalistic picture depends on not-natural elements. As a work of imitation this or any other realistic picture is only second-best to the objects it imitates. As a work of art, it is an independent object in its own right.

The harmonious quiet pervading *The Old Violin* is not produced by our reaction to the objects represented. The objects take on this quality, and we are conscious of it because of their arrangement. The same objects could be jumbled about in a restless way to create the opposite expression. (And Harnett did many such contrasting arrangements.) Thus, while we could never call *The Old Violin* an expressionistic painting, it has expressive elements.

Expressionism

Dufy's The Yellow Violin

The idea back of expressionism is that the actual appearance of objects may be distorted in any way, no matter how extreme, that the artist feels will best relay to the observer his own emotional reaction to a subject. Expressionism is usually associated with morbid, violent, or sorrowful subjects (Kokoschka's *The Tempest* in Portfolio 1 is an expressionistic painting), but it need not be. Dufy's violin is bright, vivacious, happy. The color has nothing to do with nature but everything to do with what Dufy wants to tell us. The drawing is as fluid and broken as Harnett's is concise, and hence its effect is as animated as Harnett's is serene. The notes on the sheet of music are a series of brilliant staccato accents with only the loosest connection to a readable score. Everything expresses liveliness, spontaneity, improvisation. As for its being "too easy to do," it was easy for Dufy to do in the same manner that a skilled pianist may appear to execute a particularly dashing series of runs and trills without effort.

Abstraction

Braque's Musical Forms

In spite of distortion, the objects in an expressionistic picture are usually recognizable. But in abstraction the objects tend to lose their identity as objects and to exist as pure form. Braque's *Musical Forms* is no longer a "picture of" a violin, although a violin was the point of departure for some of its most conspicuous elements. Nor is it an emotional reaction to the idea of "violin" as Dufy's is. It is purely what it is: an arrangement of lines, shapes, colors, and textures.

Beneath their differences, Braque's abstraction and Harnett's collection of realistically painted objects have strong similarities. Both arrangements are disciplined by a system of rigid straight lines, both are relieved by contrasting curved ones. The area enclosing the first five letters of the word "Journal" in the Braque is even in a location and at an angle and of a shape like the addressed envelope in the Harnett. Although this is a coincidence, it is produced by compositional demands common to both paintings. And there are circular forms in the Braque which serve the same compositional purpose as the iron ring in the Harnett. Finally, within the two schemes there is even a related interest in textures. Harnett simulates textures. Braque utilizes actual, physical ones. The charcoal lines are left grainy to reveal the texture of the canvas; the blue area is fairly thick in some parts, scrubbed thin in others for variety. The paint in the two tan areas has been scratched while wet with some comblike instrument, creating a rigid texture resembling the grain of wood but not meant to imitate it. Whatever they suggest, these textures exist for themselves rather than as adjuncts to something else, which all textures are in the Harnett. As an aside, we might mention that Harnett too, in his earlier pictures, "textured" his paint so that a match head, for instance, might be built up in relief from the surface of the canvas.

The difference between doing what Braque does and building up a match head to look like a match head or imitating the surface of an old violin to look like the surface of an old violin is the difference between realism and abstraction. Braque abandons the appearance of things because he wants to capitalize fully on the same abstract elements that interested Harnett (plus others) instead of having to disguise these abstract elements within the imitation of nature. Just why Braque chooses also the further abstraction of breaking his forms up as he does is too long a story to tell here. It is part of the story of cubism and comes in a later portfolio. But in the meantime these three violins will serve as a reminder that although the subject of this portfolio is realism, all painting, whether realistic, expressionistic, or abstract, involves the creation and arrangement of form and color according to the way the painter sees, feels, and thinks about the world.

What Is Realism?

Now "realism" is probably the broadest term in art, so broad that we must make our own working definition of it here. We will call any painting realistic in which a fairly close approximation of the look of things is retained. The realistic painter may considerably modify natural appearances, but he will stop short of the point where modification becomes distortion.

By this definition the bulk of painting is realistic (excepting modern art). But the real world to one age is not the real world to another. The world around the artist changes, not only superficially in the obvious way of different buildings, different dress, and the like, but more fundamentally, since as times change men see the world differently, think about it differently, and hence paint it differently even when they begin by imitating the look of things. We will examine eight paintings stretching across the past five hundred years and one done fifteen or thirty thousand years ago that will give a suggestion of the variety of ways men have thought about the world around them, and the corresponding variety of ways in which artists have reflected it within our definition of realism.

The End of the Middle Ages Mystical Realism

The function of art is frequently defined as the creation of order out of the chaos of human experience. This suggests that the artist creates by simplifying the material the world offers him. When the ancient Greeks created the ideal form of the Greek god, whose beauty expressed for them the ideal harmony they felt beneath the accidentals and complications of life, their point of departure was the simplification of natural forms by the elimination of these same accidentals and complications.

But the more we see of art the more we realize that there is no one way of achieving an expression of order and harmony. Van Eyck's *Saint Francis Receiving the Stigmata* (Plate 16), a painting of the Middle Ages executed a little over five hundred years ago, goes about putting the world in order in just the opposite way. Instead of simplifying, the painter multiplies detail. Paradoxical as that may sound, it was the only reasonable approach for the painter of the Middle Ages who wanted to put the world in order.

The medieval world was rich, violent, chaotic, complicated, swarming, colorful, and thoroughly contradictory. It was an age of the extremest cruelties, of the most hideous plagues, poverty, and human suffering, of tortures and maimings and slaughter. It was also an age of exquisite refinement of living, of mystical religious faith. It was an age of opulence, of cynicism and piety, grossness and elegance. Licentiousness flourished. So did the cult of chastity. As we look back on the age, it seems to have been everything at once—except humdrum.

This welter of contradictions was unified by the assumption that the universe in its totality was a divinely ordained system of parallels in contrast. In this faith the age found its harmony. Heaven balanced hell, winter balanced summer, sowing balanced reaping, birth balanced death. Each virtue balanced its corresponding vice. And in this universal harmony, ordained by God, the smallest detail of the world had its place. Nothing was accidental; everything was meaningful.

For the medieval man the world of literal fact merged with the world of spiritual miracle and was frequently identical with it. This conception of the universe is directly reflected in medieval painting and explains why the miracle of the stigmata can be represented in such uncompromisingly realistic detail without contradicting its miraculous character. The painting from which our color plate *Saint Francis Receiving the Stigmata* was made is only three inches higher than the reproduction, yet in this small area its complexity is enormous. More extraordinary yet, another version of the picture, from which the larger one was probably adapted, is less than five inches high. It is reproduced here at exact size (*Figure 2*). In this miniature version the world is represented with stagger-

John G. Johnson Collection, Philadelphia

Figure 2

Figure 3

ing completeness; it is compressed into a few square inches without any effect of crowding or jumbling. There are trees, flowers, crags, boulders, and pebbles. There is a river, a spring with its rocky basin of crystalline water. There are hills, clouds, and birds; a city with men on foot and on horseback around its gates; there are other cities in the distance. There are roads and paths, a boatload of men. Lichens grow in miniature on the miniature boulders and—so small that they are virtually invisible until magnified—there are woodsmen bearing loads of faggots in the hills. Enlarged four times, a detail of the upper left corner shows a man and a boy on a rocky path and a crow or some similar bird on the topmost branch of a tree, with other birds in the air around it (*Figure 3*).

But breath-taking microscopic execution is not in itself of any esthetic merit. After all, dressed fleas can be purchased for a few cents in curio shops, and the Lord's Prayer engraved on the head of a pin is a famous sideshow exhibit. Certainly this tiny picture with its infinitely tiny detail was painted with the help of a powerful lens; as a tour de force this execution is fascinating in itself, but in itself it could never have made this work of art into anything more than an amazing piece of stunt painting. What is meaningful is that the painter has combined the myriad details of the world into a picture where the total effect is one of unity rather than confusion, a world where rocks, grass, foliage, cloth, hair, and flesh retain their individuality and yet share a common quality of gentleness in the even flow of light that bathes the universe. The head of the saint can be covered with a dime, yet when it is enlarged eleven times (*Figure 4*) we see that each bristle on the cheek, chin, and upper lip has been painted individually, that on the forehead and against the sky, represented in single strokes of the brush as sure and certain as if they had been painted at full scale, there are individual hairs or small locks springing from the scalp with the same energy and vitality that invests the whole picture with an extraordinary sense of life. But, again, it is this same sense of life that is remarkable, not the incredible technical means by which it is achieved. Whether the head of the saint is the size of a dime or the size of a dinner plate, it is a solid and forthright presentation of a person who exists with utterly convincing reality.

Then does the miniature scale of the picture serve no function at all? There may have been a practical reason for its size; this is not known. In any case, it is also true that here the eye rests on an entire world at once. The precision of minute realistic detail intensifies our reaction to the various objects by investing them with a magic concentration. Yet this could have been as true of a much larger version also, while the

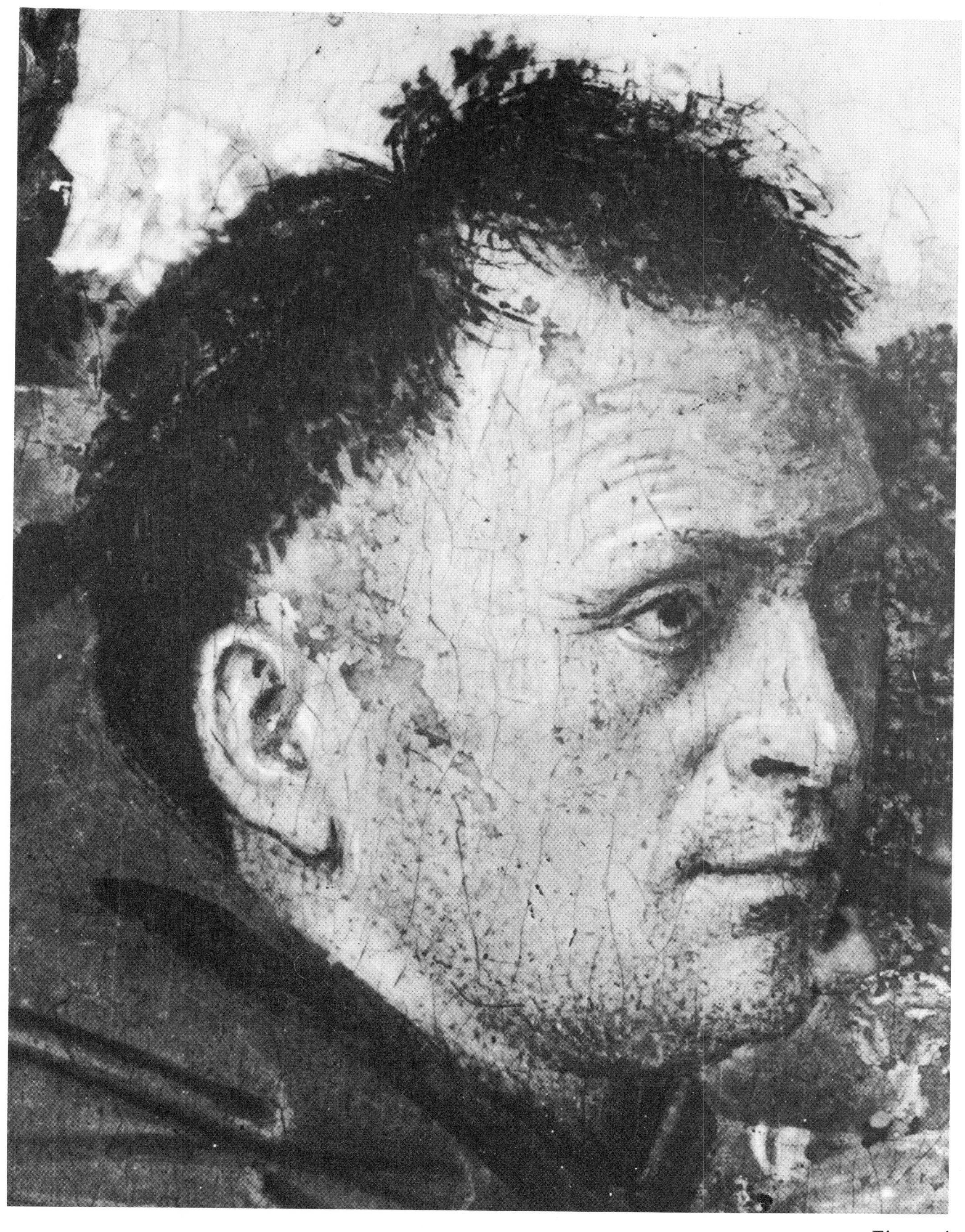

Figure 4

Figure 5

microscopic scale of this one may be distracting because we continue to be fascinated by its technical marvelousness. The important point is that this medieval philosopher has seen the world as a place where every detail around him takes on spiritual significance because it has its place in the universal harmony. Detail by detail the picture is an assemblage of commonplace objects painted quite literally—even, some critics have found, rather dryly. But as a whole the effect is not commonplace but miraculous. If any element in the picture is out of key it is, paradoxically, the un-commonplace one of the apparition of the Cross. Against the elegant complication of the city, against the vivacity of the crowds of men and horses, the pattern of the rock ledges, and the shining water with its boat, the one obviously miraculous element, the Cross, seems extraneous (*Figure 5*). Its presence is not necessary to complete the impression of reverent spirituality already conveyed through the contradictory means of extreme realism. An age made up of contradictions achieved this final one in its painting.

The Renaissance Ideal Realism

When the picture we have just seen was painted near the end of the Middle Ages, "the age of faith" had already given way in Italy to a period better described as an age of curiosity: the Renaissance. The fact that a thing existed was no longer any assurance that it had its own ready-made pigeonhole in an all-inclusive system. The Middle Ages gave meaning to the world by filing every individual part of the universal clutter around us into a systematic harmony that already existed. But renaissance man sought to discover a new harmony, more earthly, with himself as its center.

In painting, this new attitude first took the form of passionate curiosity about the world. Artists dissected corpses to learn anatomy and turned mathematician to codify the laws of perspective. They discovered that spiritually they were more closely related to the artists who had created the gods of Greece and Rome than they were to the artists of the immediate past. They began to study the remains of classical antiquity, reviving its idealism and combining with it the factualism of their new knowledge.

The result was an art cultivating dignity, elegance, grace, and intellectual breadth. Raphael's portrait *Giuliano de' Medici, Duke of Nemours* (Plate 17), has all these qualities even though the subject himself did not.

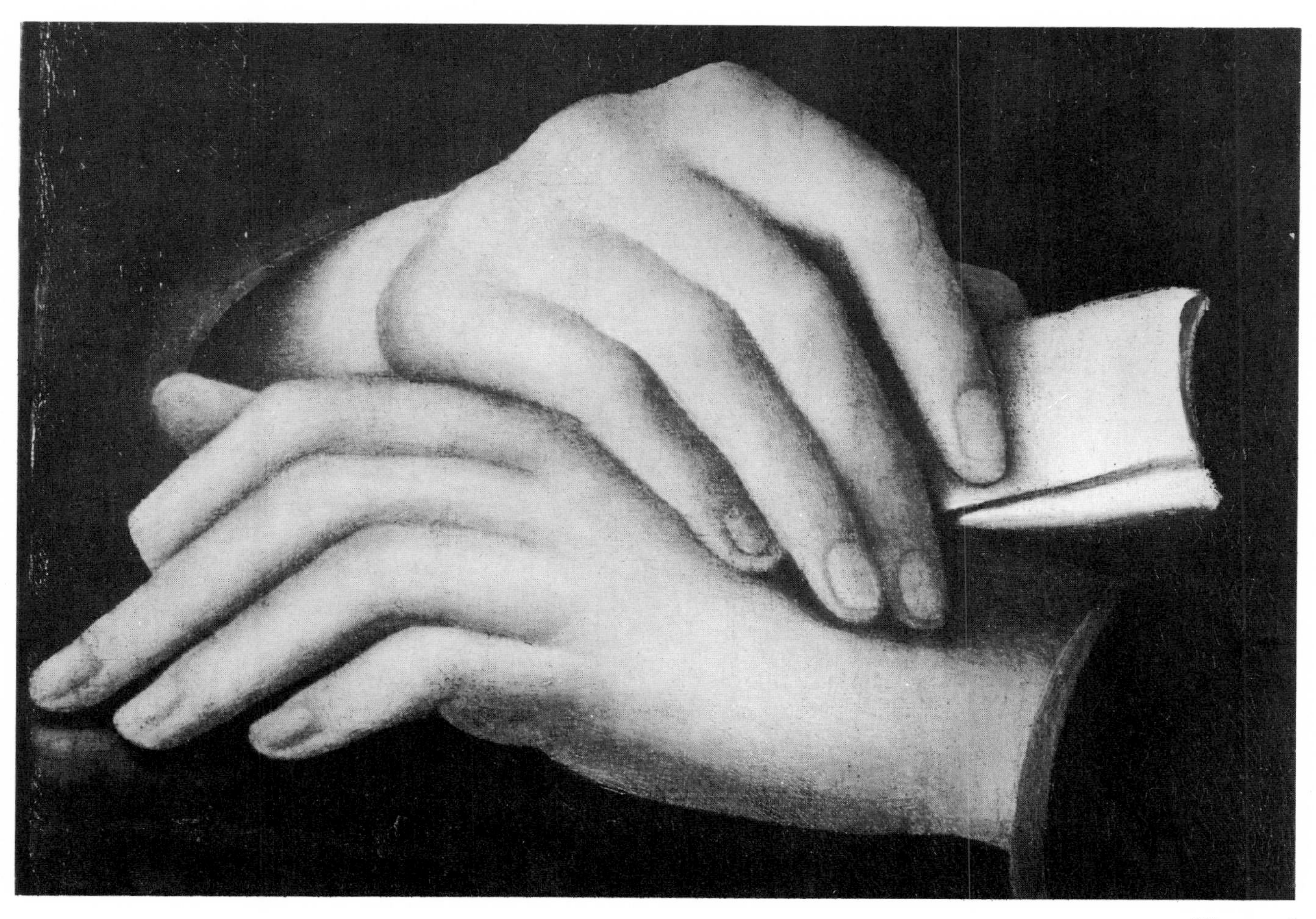

Figure 6

Raphael's intention is less to interpret his sitter's personality than to invest him with the qualities the age most admired. Whereas the forms in the Van Eyck are multitudinous, in the Raphael they are few. Whereas Van Eyck's forms are complicated, Raphael's are simplified. Whereas Van Eyck intensifies detail, Raphael eliminates it. We can sum up these differences by comparing the treatment of the saint's habit in the Van Eyck with that of the fashionable costume in the Raphael.

Giuliano is wearing an elaborate costume and a hat of spectacular shape. The saint, on the other hand, wears only a sacklike habit with a hood, or cowl.

Yet from all the elaborations of Giuliano's costume Raphael has designed a quiet pattern of half a dozen restrained silhouettes spotted by an occasional subdued accent. But Van Eyck has painted the simple robe of his saint as a multiplication of folds that keep it busy from top to bottom. Likewise, Raphael chooses a curtain for his background and keeps it devoid of incident while Van Eyck gives us all the world behind the hill where his saint kneels. It has been necessary for Raphael to draw the curtain a bit to one side to reveal the Castel Sant' Angelo in the background, a specific reference connected with Giuliano, but this bit of landscape is treated simply. In this area, larger than the entire surface of the Van Eyck, there is less detail than in a square inch of cityscape in the earlier picture (*Figure 5*). The same contrast is apparent if we compare the hands of the prince (*Figure 6*) with those of the saint (*Figure 5*). And finally in the heads the antithesis is complete. Whereas Van Eyck sought to reproduce a head down to the last bristle of the beard, Raphael used his model for a simplified, idealized head (*Figure 7*)—within the limitations of preserving an adequate likeness—where the subordinate parts of the natural object are not reproduced in detail but are modified by the elimination of details.

Mere elimination of detail is a simple enough process and in itself has no more meaning than the opposite, "dressed flea" approach of microscopic imitation. But Raphael's forms are not only simplified; they are beautifully ordered. In short, the difference between the Van Eyck and the Raphael is this: the medieval painter seeks to give meaning to the complication of the world; the renaissance painter seeks to clarify a meaning obscured by it.

Yet realistic representation of worldly objects is their common point of departure.

The Seventeenth Century: Dramatic Realism

Nothing we have said about the five pictures discussed so far changes the fact that when the average person looks at a picture he is not concerned with the spirit of the age that produced it, or the means the artist used to make his effect, or with anything except what the picture is about. And for him what the picture is about means what is going on in it, and the more that goes on the better he likes it.

He wants to experience vicariously some pictured event as if he were there. He is not interested in philosophy or composition or inner meanings. He wants something to be happening, something amusing, something touching, or something big and exciting.

This yearning on the part of the observer to share a pictured experience is capitalized on by most bad painters and some very good ones. It is made the most of in Rubens's *Prometheus Bound* (Plate 18), where we are treated in as direct a way as possible to the spectacle of a giant writhing in agony as an eagle devours his liver. Prometheus, who stole fire from Olympus and gave it to mankind, was punished by the gods in the manner pictured. His liver was devoured daily; nightly it grew back, making his punishment eternal.

This is rich subject matter for a painter who wants to overpower the spectator. Rubens offers us no invitation to divine meditation nor to the contemplation of harmonious order. Here

Figure 7

is art of the kind that seeks to astonish. The spectator must, first of all, be shocked into an emotional response. He must not be allowed to pass by; no chance may be taken with his possible indifference. To attract him any means is legitimate, no matter how spectacular, how violent, or, in some cases, how false.

Now, the quickest and surest way to shock is through physical experience. And since the painter who approaches us through astonishment cannot touch us with live coals, nor dash us with cold water, nor strike us a blow, he does the next best thing: he creates astonishing images so convincing that we share the pictured physical experience. In the case of this Rubens painting the physical experience is at least obvious, but the same idea can be applied in ways not quite so direct. Flesh or cloth or water or wind or hair or feathers or rock may be so painted that they stir our associations of physical experience rather than our ideological ones. An angel flying through the air is something we have never seen (any more than we have ever seen a giant chained to a rock), but if it can be painted so that the flesh and cloth and hair and feathers are like physically real experiences to us we are going to believe in the existence of that angel.

At least that is the intention behind dramatized realism of this kind. The appeal to our own physical experience of painful or pleasurable sensations is going to be most effective to the extent that the image is most tangible. For that reason there is no idealization in the figure of the powerful man who plays Prometheus. This is, actually, as naturalistic a painting as we have seen so far, for all its illusion of tempestuous drama and its fantastic subject. If Rubens had been a degree less skillful in maintaining the illusion we would find ourselves imagining the model posed in the studio, illuminated by a spotlight and complaining that his left leg was going to sleep.

Why did this development occur in painting? A corresponding one—as is always true—was taking place in the other arts, particularly in architecture, much of which shared the elaborated and sensationalized character of painting. The seventeenth century placed its faith in worldly power. It did not really believe in miracles as the medieval world did; it did not really hope to discover harmony beneath confusion, as the Renaissance did. When miracles were represented they had to be shown in terms of acute physical experience to be credible on any score, and when the ideal was represented, it was shown as a nostalgic recall of a dream-world—and even this world of dream was presented in terms of the world of tangible fact.

Does this mean that the *Prometheus* is a "bad" painting? Certainly not. It is a great painting. Beneath its surface emotionalism the effects are calculated with shrewd objectivity. And, as in other pictures, we may find additional enjoyment here as we watch the painter work out his melodrama, even while we respond to it emotionally.

In an age of such violence and novelty as our own, people are not easy to astonish. But the power of an image is so great that the *Prometheus* continues to astonish even in an age when we would expect it to pale in comparison with newsreels and photographs of current events astonishing and painful beyond belief. Perhaps that is the clue to the picture's effectiveness: it is not beyond belief. It brings the event close to us, makes us part of itself, in a way that factual records do not.

Velazquez: The Eye as a Lens

The seventeenth century produced armies of painters who were under no technical limitations at all; painters who could draw any figure, from any angle, in any curious or distorted attitude, whether or not they had anything to say. It is not surprising that the age produced the most absolute realist of them all: Velazquez.

If ever painting, in its purest definition as the controlled application of paint to canvas, can be its own excuse for being, it is so in the art of Velazquez. *The Maids of Honor* (Plate 19) shows a little princess of the Spanish court attended by various ladies in waiting while, to one side in the background, the painter himself is at work on the picture we are seeing. Farther back, reflected in a mirror, the king and queen watch him at work (*Figure 8*). The painting gives the impression of being executed in realistic detail, but when we look at a section of it we discover that is not true. Here is a new kind of realistic vision. Whereas Van Eyck would have painted individual hairs, Velazquez paints not a single strand or even a definable mass. Velazquez is not painting hair; he is painting the light reflected onto the retina of his eye by a substance that happens to be hair. He translates this reflected light into pigmented tones, giving us only the impression of the color, texture, and form of hair in terms of light (*Figure 9*). He does the same with the ornament of ribbon at one temple and at the neck of the dress. We could not describe these objects in precise detail because we are not familiar with them as specific objects. We know them only as light reflected over the considerable distance between the painter and his model, a distance that reduces the object to spots of color with concentrations of lighter and darker tones in highlights and shadows. In this kind of painting we see more than the artist puts there. Cover the upper and lower parts of the nose and you will see that its bridge is not described as form. We supply the missing description, just as we supply the individual hairs because we know they are there; just as we supply the lower lid of the little girl's far eye because we know it is there, though hardly suggested; just as we supply the division between the neck and the jaw near the hair, although as far as descriptive painting of form is concerned that area is largely blank. On the other side of the face the dividing line between cheek and hair is so softened that in places it cannot be precisely determined—but again we supply it. Velazquez paints the light reflected by an object across the distance between him and the object; he does not paint what memory

Photo by MAS

Figure 8

or close-range inspection tells him is present. If he had been painting the city in the background of the Van Eyck he would have painted it in blurs and spots, which is all the eye can see of a city at such a distance. He would never have painted the individual bristles in the beard of the saint, even if he had been painting the head at life size, since the eye does not see such details clearly except at very close range. Van Eyck paints the details of all objects as they would appear on close inspection; Velazquez paints detail only to the degree that it is visible from where he, and hence the observer, stands.

The beauty of Velazquez's realism is its consistency. As objects recede into the distance of his pictures and become more vague, as they come into the foreground and become more sharply defined, every brush stroke, every tone, every color modulation is in perfect relationship—as a reflection of light—to every other.

All this sounds like the ultimate degree in the

Photo by Anderson

Figure 9

mere imitation of nature. As a technician is Velazquez only a lens equipped with a paint brush? No. He selects, he modifies, he eliminates meaningless or confusing accidentals, he slightly heightens or lowers intensities of light or shadow to create a world of subtler visual harmonies than the one that serves him as a model. He creates a luminous world with its own abstract beauty in its order, its harmony, its consistency, its perfect relationship between every nuance of descriptive color.

Still, optical delight even at its maximum cannot explain the enduring appeal of Velazquez as an expressive painter rather than a supertechnician. Where does his expressive quality lie? It cannot be discovered in terms of Rubens's effulgent vigor. By this standard Velazquez's religious paintings are meaningless collections of effigies, and his allegorical or mythological subjects end up as prosaic groups of patient models, beautifully painted. His expressive quality lies at the opposite pole: from Velazquez's world all passionate intensity, all mystery or symbolism, and all intellectual philosophizing have been distilled as impurities. The images exist for themselves, always once removed from us, separated by an invisible barrier behind which they stand regarding us impassively, complete in their own being. When Velazquez paints an image of the Madonna we must accept it as the Madonna, just as literally as we accept, in *The Maids of Honor*, the room with the little princess and her entourage. His art poses no question and suggests no paths to solutions; it presents us with a *fait accompli*, as if the question having been asked and the solution found we need concern ourselves with neither, content to accept without query the answer Velazquez offers without comment.

The Eighteenth Century: Reality in Pots and Pans

So far in our chronological sequence we have discussed a mystical universe, an Italian aristocrat, a Titan, and a princess as realistic images expressive of their times. After a list of such elevated subjects the appearance of three apples, two pears, a mug, and a knife on a stone ledge might be taken to indicate that a new century has lost its sense of the grand and the noble. This is not so. In this picture the eighteenth century is discovering that nobility can exist in the commonplace. We all know that near the end of the century in France noble heads were chopped off by the common man in a not very noble extension of this idea.

The events of 1776 in our own country were a social manifestation involving the philosophical idea that nobility exists in the simplest things and the simplest people. Without exaggerating too much we could argue that the Declaration of Independence and Chardin's *Still Life* (Plate 20) are first cousins under the skin.

Still-life painting is boring to many people, because it is too often merely imitative. But a good still life can also be an expressive picture, and the range of expression can be fairly wide. (We have already seen one expression of it in the harmonious quiet of Harnett's *The Old Violin.*) Its range cannot compare with that of landscape or the human figure, but even so it would be possible to tell the history of painting, on a reduced scale, in still life alone. Until Chardin, though, we would normally find still life either an incidental part of a larger picture or, when a picture in itself, an ornamental display of technical skill as in a canvas by Jan Davidsz. de Heem, one of the most influential seventeenth-century painters of still life (*Figure 10*). But with Chardin still life becomes an expressive vehicle in its own right.

The objects in Chardin's paintings are very real. As far as accuracy of drawing is concerned they are photographic—which of course is not enough. In painting, however, they have some of the same departures from exact imitation that we commented on in Velazquez's work—adjustment of light and dark tones, modulations in color, a general harmonizing of the ob-

The Metropolitan Museum of Art

Figure 10

jects with one another. But the two painters are not alike in effect. We have said that Velazquez was painting light. Chardin is painting form. Everything he does is directed toward one end, the expression of the weight, solidity, and repose that he feels in the objects he selects to paint (*Figure 11*). Even the paint itself is heavier, richer, more firmly applied than Velazquez's.

The seven objects in our illustration are arranged very simply on the homely shelf but very rightly. There are no set rules for this kind of pictorial composition and thus no really good way to explain why one succeeds or fails. The objects are placed in a kind of balance that cannot be calculated but can only "feel" right or wrong. The simpler such an arrangement is and the fewer the objects included in it the more difficult is the problem of adjustment of the parts to one another. You can test this arrangement by imagining it without the knife. Immediately the mug is divorced from the other objects. Or if we substitute another apple for the upright pear or shift its position so that it leans toward the center of the picture rather than toward the left, we discover that we have to make other changes to compensate for the disturbed relationships.

Chardin's humble objects appear to be casually placed. Novelty or flamboyance would be the most disharmonious possible element in such a picture. The objects are intended to appeal through their simplicity and their everydayness, in which Chardin's (seemingly) simple, straightforward presentation is in contrast with the elegance and artificiality of fashionable eighteenth-century painting just as the idea of the ordinary man's innate virtue was contrasted with the artificiality of the fashionable world. It makes no difference whether "natural" man turned out to be as noble as the philosophers hoped. It was a noble conception, it was in the air, and it found its way into Chardin's painting.

The Nineteenth Century: Anecdotal Realism

The nineteenth century was of all centuries the practical one, the common-sense one, the respectable middle-class one. Whatever other qualities it had, its life was centered around this substantial core. The ideal of "natural no-

Figure 11

Figure 12

bility" became in reality frequently more vulgar than ideal. In an age that was what we call "realistic about things" in its daily philosophy, realistic painting flourished over a range as wide as the century's own attitude toward the daily world: from crass to profound in its understanding of human life.

Gérôme's *The Duel After the Masquerade* (Plate 21) is at neither the top nor the bottom of this range. We can begin to see just where it belongs by comparing its realism to Chardin's. When we say of the Chardin, "A pear on the left and a mug on the right bound three apples, another pear, and a knife on a stone shelf" we have said little about the picture. Its meaning lies elsewhere, as we have tried to explain. But when we say of the Gérôme, "After a duel in a snowy open space within a park, a male figure costumed as a seventeenth-century burgher supports another costumed as Pierrot, who, wounded, collapses as a third, costumed as an oriental potentate, examines the wound, and a fourth in a rich velvet cloak clutches his head in grief (*Figure 12*); to the right the successful dueler, costumed as an American Indian, leaves the field accompanied by his second, costumed as Harlequin" we have described the essence of the picture, if we add that technically it is a brilliantly performed exercise. The picture is an anecdote. The anecdote may be pathetic, but the picture is not interpretative. It neither enlarges nor intensifies our experience. We cannot find anything else for the picture to "say" unless it says, as we already know, that when young men get into a fight after a dance someone is likely to get hurt. With the young men in costume there is an element of fantasy for frosting. In other words, the picture is superficial.

This does not mean that a duel after a masquerade couldn't serve as a subject for a moving interpretation of some aspect of life. The anecdotal quality is inherent in the treatment, not in the subject. As mighty a subject as the Crucifixion could be reduced to anecdotal level by similar treatment—and has been, more than once. Any meaning we read into the picture must come from our reaction to the anecdote;

it is not implicit in Gérôme's telling of it. And in the words "telling of it" we indicate that the approach is essentially literary, rather than painterly. The picture is an illustration, taking second place to something else rather than existing in its own creative right.

The painting's shortcomings are typical of nineteenth-century academic painting, the painting of the popular, successful artist who pleased the public because his art was easily understood and undemanding. But in making all these objections we are not insisting that every painting should be a great one. Painting at a second level has its place too, if it does not pretend to be anything else. If we accept the Gérôme as a stunning technical rendering, a pleasant bit of decorative color, a graceful combination of attractive figures, then it is an enjoyable picture. It hangs in a gallery full of nineteenth-century paintings of very high caliber and holds its own very well among them.

Realism and the Poetry of Daily Life

It is usually easier to explain what is wrong with a picture than to show what makes it good. This is because the better a picture is the more likely it is to communicate in terms that cannot be expressed as well in any other medium. This is true of other art forms too. What Shakespeare says in *Hamlet*, for instance, has not been said as well in a painting. Similarly, what Thomas Eakins says in his portrait *Miss Van Buren* (Plate 22) is said so completely in terms of a realistic image that when we come to discuss it the temptation is to say no more than "just look at it!" The picture is one of those great ones whose meaning is as obvious as it is unexplainable in specific comment.

Certain of its many virtues are explainable, however. As a realistic drawing (that is, as the expression by lines and shadows of a three-dimensional form on a two-dimensional surface) it is superbly skillful. Eakins is completely master of the craft of realistic drawing, which he inherits fully developed from the centuries of painters who worked before him. As a realistic painting (that is, as a drawing that includes the re-creation of the colors of the represented objects) the picture is equally good. As creative realism, in its selection and modification from the visual material it uses, it employs some devices we can be specific about.

The sitter has, first of all, been posed in an attitude natural in effect and expressively characteristic. From this advantageous beginning Eakins goes on to exaggerations of the natural contrasts between light and shade. Without getting theatrical he creates a spotlight effect, a formula used by hundreds of painters. (Rembrandt used it most insistently.) By its use Eakins directs our attention to the salient passages of his subject, intensifying their effect by displaying them brightly against other passages that are relatively blotted out. But he does this so subtly that we are not conscious of the exaggeration, as Rembrandt makes us conscious of intensification for a more emotionalized statement. Eakins does not want to emotionalize his subject; the mood is one of contemplation but not of mystery. This mood is stated in the color too, which is modified away from unexpected combinations or full intensities.

But not one of these devices is original with Eakins; we could find all of them combined similarly in any number of pictures that are nothing but proficient demonstrations of technique. Is the Eakins a greater picture because it does the conventional thing but does it better? No. Eakins employs these familiar devices with maximum skill, but there remains an intangible quality in the art of every great painter, one that makes the difference in Eakins's case between this image of Miss Van Buren, which is so vital, and an image that is a lifeless effigy.

Whatever this intangible quality is, with Eakins it has to do with honesty. Feature by feature Miss Van Buren's face is not a beautiful one (*Figure 13*). It is even rather plain. But she is not glamourized or flattered. In terms of the

Figure 13

average portrait, where the purpose is to produce an acceptably accurate likeness as beautified as possible, Eakins's picture would be mercilessly and pointlessly realistic. But a great Eakins portrait is neither glamourization nor documentation. It is a great picture finding within the substantial everyday world poetry of such strength that it needs no bolstering up by prettification or ornament.

If we could explain in words exactly where this poetry lies the picture would lose part of its reason for being. It is simply there, stated in terms of pigment on canvas. Comparing this picture with the others we have been discussing, we see that it is not idealized (like the Raphael), nor melodramatized (like the Rubens), nor objective (like the Velazquez). Its everydayness is related to Chardin's; its greatest contrast is with the Van Eyck. Whereas Van Eyck saw every fragment of the world taking on meaning as part of a great established scheme of things, Eakins sees that each fragment of reality must be accepted for itself, for whatever meaning it has in itself, independent of a divinely organized, an idealized, or a dramatized world.

This idea is stated more emphatically in our next illustration, Manet's *Boating* (Plate 23).

Realism as a Fragment of Experience

Boating is a picture put together as if the subject had been caught by accident, in a snapshot, as if it were a fragment of a larger scene. The effect is to increase our feeling of intimacy and participation in the picture. Harmonizing with this apparently offhand composition, the technique is sketchy. A sort of shorthand is used for the eyes and other features, for the details of clothes, particularly the hat and veil of the woman (*Figure 14*), for the expanse of water.

Living in a century when science had demonstrated that no one man can begin to know the universe, Manet was not interested in trying to make any universal statement, ideal or other-

Figure 14

wise. He seems to say: "Here is a fragment of the world, a moment, an instant in a day, to be appreciated for its own sake, without too much concern over its place in the vast, incomprehensible scheme of things."

This approach is typical of impressionism, a form of realism that appeals because it so frequently discovers for us an idyllic quality in the commonplace. In the hands of trivial painters it can be most trivial and fragmentary indeed, but in the hands of serious and sensitive painters like Renoir, Degas (Plates 4 and 5, Portfolio 1), and Manet it shows us that reality in commonplace terms has importance. It tells us that although the universal scheme of things may be beyond our comprehension, our moment of it can be understood in terms of feeling and sentiment.

Some critics and painters, turning prophet, believe that impressionism is the last flower of realism and that realism must now give way while the painter explores other means of expressing the world of emotion and intellect, as he has been doing recently in the various kinds of painting we lump together under the label "modern art." There are strong arguments to support this idea, even though it is offered in rather short perspective. We will have a chance to examine it further in our next two portfolios, Expressionism and Abstraction. In the meantime, dropping back fifteen or thirty thousand years, we will conclude with a few words on the oldest paintings in the world.

Prehistory and What Is Real

The paintings we have been seeing and the meanings we have ascribed to them were parts of civilizations whose histories we know, whose philosophies have been written down in words and expressed in music, architecture, drama, and the other arts as well as in painting. But there is one magnificent group of paintings that stands as the only record of the world that produced them. These are the cave paintings of southern France and northern Spain.

The tribal artists who decorated the walls of the ritual cave of Lascaux in southern France must be included among the great painters of all time. Aside from their fascinating evocation of a life infinitely removed from ours, one which they bring overwhelmingly close, these are great paintings. They would be great paintings if they had been done yesterday.

They swarm over the walls of the cave, brilliantly fresh, magnificently alive. Our detail shows two bison (Plate 24). How passionately the artist has observed these animals! He sums up the idea of "bison" in the most acute and economical way—the powerful forequarters, the small, taut hindquarters, the contrasting bony delicacy of hoofs and shins, the brutishness of the head, the menacing curve of the horns. Everything is understood in its essence, and the essential quality is expressed by the most effective degree of emphasis.

Are these paintings realistic by our definition? Do they hold close to an accurate reproduction of visual fact? Certainly the artists' intention was to recreate the animals. We must remember that these cave paintings were made and seen by men who had no conception of the deadly accuracy painting would later achieve, not to mention photography. They must have seemed real in something like an illusionistic sense.

If they had been painted today we might call these bison expressionistic. The exaggeration very nearly reaches the point of distortion. A contemporary artist painting in this manner would be working from the consciously held theory that the image would be most intense if every element—forequarters, hindquarters, hoofs and shins, head, horns—were distorted to intensify its character. The power, the tautness, the brutishness, the menace, the delicacy of the various parts of the animal would be analyzed in relation to one another. Did the cave painter analyze first, then paint? It is easy to imagine him as a more primitive creator than he may have been. Of course we cannot know. But the images these artists have left are too deft and too consistently skilled to be the product of some freakish natural talents. They are real, less in the sense of looking like the animals (although they do that) than in the sense of expressing their emotional realness as men knew them. And to the men whose world is echoed in these caves the animal had an importance beyond comparison with any element in our own world. The animal's flesh was food and very nearly the only food. Its hide was clothing; its bone was the raw material for tools. The hunter's power over animals was quite fundamentally a matter of his life or death. The paintings were adjuncts to ritual, not decorations in living quarters. These rituals probably had to do with magical influence to aid the hunter. The idea that possession of an image of a loved or hated person can give the possessor power over that person still exists in voodoo today.

It is no wonder that the cave paintings are still invested with so powerful an emotional reality. This emotional reality, sometimes departing far from visual reality, is the preoccupation of the expressionistic artist today and the next portfolio will be devoted to this subject.

Notes on the Painters

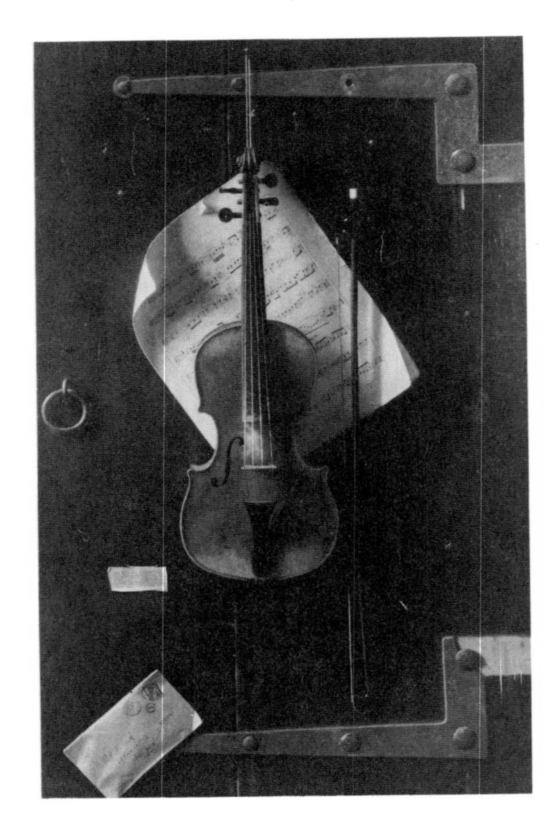

William Michael Harnett, 1848-1892, American

13. THE OLD VIOLIN, 1886

Oil on canvas. Height 38". William J. Williams, Cincinnati, Ohio

Harnett was born in Ireland but came to this country as a child and lived in Philadelphia. The acute naturalism of his painting has always had an immediate fascination for the layman, but critics have not always been able to see beneath it. At the moment Harnett has risen decisively in critical esteem, and it appears that his ambiguous position between popular art and fine art has finally been resolved with the recognition that he is one of those rare artists who fuse the two.

Harnett sold his pictures for as much as $10,000, and during a European sojourn he had a picture accepted for exhibition at the Paris Salon. At that time (1885) the Salon had not lost prestige with the general public, and in America especially it was unquestioned as the goal every painter naturally yearned to achieve. Harnett's painting might not have made the grade among the swarms of prettified nudes and grandiose historical anecdotes that were standard Salon fare if he had not assembled some rather more elegant objects than usual into a large arrangement suggestive of eighteenth-century French decorative panels. (This picture, *After the Hunt*, now hangs in the California Palace of the Legion of Honor in San Francisco.) But he was less at home, and less original, in such a demonstration piece than in a sharply adjusted composition of ordinary objects like *The Old Violin*.

Harnett's rediscovery by contemporary critics is related to his superficial resemblance to two recent vogues: first, to surrealism, which is so frequently based on microscopically naturalistic reproduction of familiar objects in fantastic juxtaposition; second, to the *Merz-bild*, or "trash picture," a concretion of miscellaneous fragments of paper, wood, metal, or anything else pasted or otherwise held together on a surface. Collage is a more restrained application of the same idea, that is, that colors and textures ordinarily taken for granted assume new meanings when moved from their familiar context into an unrelated one. (See also Braque, below.)

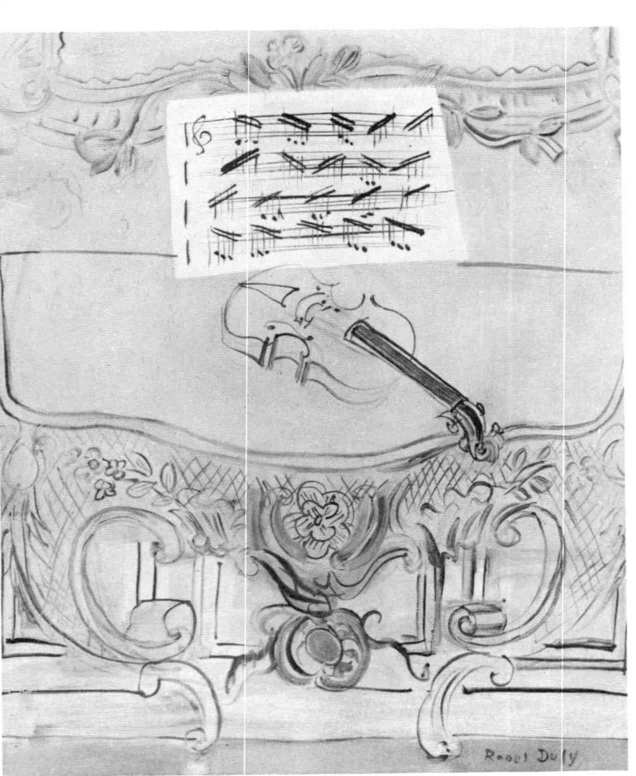

Raoul Dufy, 1877-1953, French

14. THE YELLOW VIOLIN, 1949

Oil on canvas. Height 39⅜". Mr. and Mrs. Samuel J. Zacks, Toronto

Dufy was one of the young painters exhibiting together in 1905 called the *Fauves*, or Wild Beasts. The name, given in derision, has stuck even though it is inappropriate. The fauves painted in pure bright colors vigorously applied, but their work is hypercivilized rather than savage. Matisse proved to be the most durable and inventive member of the group. His range is wider than Dufy's, but not even Matisse excels Dufy in Dufy's chosen manner, one of fashionable vivacity, at once suave and brilliant.

Next to Matisse, the best known fauve name is that of Georges Braque. Braque, however, soon abandoned the spontaneous emotional approach of fauvism and shifted to the more purely intellectualized one of cubism. In the first half of the twentieth century fauvism and cubism represent respectively the romantic and classic divergence that has been characteristic of French painting for a hundred and fifty years.

Georges Braque, born 1881, French

15. MUSICAL FORMS, 1913

Oil, pencil, and charcoal on canvas. Height 36¼". The Philadelphia Museum of Art, Louise and Walter Arensberg Collection

Braque shares with Picasso a pre-eminent position among cubist painters; many critics feel that of them all he has most sensitively explored its possibilities. Picasso has most dramatically adapted cubism to a variety of expressions, but Braque has more subtly followed its original intentions.

Cubism developed so rapidly (around 1906 and 1907) that in retrospect it seems to have been spontaneously self-generated. Actually it was invented by Picasso, Braque, and certainly Juan Gris among others, in such close association that nobody remembers exactly which ideas were contributed by which members of the group.

Among the offshoots of cubism was the collage. A collage may be a composition made up entirely of paper, cardboard, sandpaper, cloth, and similar materials. Such materials may also be combined with painted areas and passages of drawing, usually in charcoal. *Musical Forms* is not a collage; everything is painted or drawn, but the blue painted areas might well have been pasted paper without much difference in effect, as could the brownish textured area.

Braque used collage with particular felicity, but like the other artists who first used it he has long since abandoned it to the novelty craftsmen and the art classroom, where it is used as an exercise to develop sensitivity to surface textures. Since his experiments with collage, variations in surface texture have been an integral part of Braque's composition. His paint texture from one passage to another may change as distinctively as if he were still working in a variety of materials.

Jan van Eyck, active by 1422—died 1441, Flemish

16. SAINT FRANCIS RECEIVING THE STIGMATA, ABOUT 1438

Oil on wood. Height 11". The Sabauda Gallery, Turin

Photo by Anderson

Jan van Eyck also painted the double portrait of Giovanni Arnolfini and his wife Giovanna Cenami illustrated in Portfolio 1, where comment was made on him and his brother Hubert in the Notes on the Painters. Since each work by the Van Eycks either remained in the spot for which it was painted or early found its way into the great collections of western Europe and Russia, it is remarkable that America, where collecting began so late, should have any Van Eycks at all. Another version of the painting *Saint Francis Receiving the Stigmata*, the one from which our details are taken, is in Philadelphia; in the National Gallery in Washington an *Annunciation*; and in the Metropolitan another *Annunciation* that may be Hubert's, a magnificent *Crucifixion*, and a *Last Judgment*. In 1955 the Frick Collection in New York acquired from a European collection *Virgin and Child with Saints and a Carthusian Donor* by Jan van Eyck and a follower, Petrus Christus.

Raphael, 1483-1520, Italian

17. GIULIANO DE' MEDICI, ABOUT 1515

Tempera and oil on canvas. Height 32¾". The Metropolitan Museum of Art

Raphael is usually accepted as the painter in whose work the renaissance ideal of order and harmony was finally attained. The grace, elegance, and aplomb of his art also characterized his life. He went from one success to another without difficulty or interruption.

He began his career in provincial Umbria in central Italy under the proficient but rather saccharine painter Perugino. As little more than a schoolboy he was already so skillful an imitator of Perugino's style that his earliest paintings are easy to confuse with his master's. His best work from this period, however, has a lyrical quality beyond anything Perugino achieved, and some will always prefer these youthful works to any of his other achievements.

In 1504 at the age of twenty-one he shifted his activities to Florence where he was quickly affected by the more solidly articulated style of the Florentine painters. His work gained in force without losing its native Umbrian grace.

His progressive successes led him directly into the service of the Pope himself. Moving now to Rome, he executed a series of impressive frescoes in the Vatican and numerous portraits and subject pictures of varying quality. He assimilated the Roman intellectual climate and became a painter of grand and sometimes grandiose forms. But when he sought to achieve something of the titanic power of Michelangelo Raphael at last met his match; for the first time he appears to be striving beyond his reach. But his best work in Rome shows him as a designer of consummate skill in compositional structures on a noble scale. And in his Roman portraits, of which *Giuliano de' Medici* is one, there is an impressive advance in psychological penetration.

Peter Paul Rubens, 1577-1640, Flemish

18. PROMETHEUS BOUND, 1612–18

Oil on canvas. Height 8'. The Philadelphia Museum of Art, Wilstach Collection

Rubens, even more than Raphael, lived a life that could serve as a model for an ideal one. Handsome, vigorous, intelligent, talented, and with the good sense to enjoy these natural endowments, he reaped all their advantages without, apparently, any suggestion of acquisitiveness, opportunism, or other littleness. He was sought after by the great and powerful of the world, respected and admired by all men, and loved by the two women who were his wives and the mothers of his children. He was not only a painter; he also served his country on diplomatic missions. He lived to the age of sixty-three, and if his life included certain sorrows, they served only to complete him as a human being.

From this triumphant existence emerged an art consistently triumphant in mood. For an age that adored magnificence Rubens created images of an opulence so fleshy that less lusty spirits sometimes find them unpalatable. The typical Rubens woman is a dewy giantess crowned with shimmering masses of golden hair; her male counterpart is a great full-bodied athlete surging with life, glowing with health—and sometimes running to fat.

Rubens produced vast quantities of painting. The demand for his work was so great that it was usual for him to receive orders for paintings in lots. He established a studio with so many assistants that it is often called his factory. He was, however, scrupulously honest in telling his customers just what portions of the painting were his own. In an inventory of his best paintings, made in 1618, Rubens mentions the *Prometheus* of our illustration, calling it "an original by my own hand, the eagle done by Snyders." Snyders, Rubens's best bird painter, is also a painter of considerable reputation in his own right.

Diego Rodríguez de Silva y Velazquez, 1599-1660, Spanish

19. THE MAIDS OF HONOR, 1656

Oil on canvas. Height 10'5¼". The Prado Museum, Madrid

Photo by Anderson

Velazquez is an exception among painters in that his work has always been popular—and popular for legitimate reasons.

The Maids of Honor (*Las Meninas*) is the most complicated picture he ever painted. The typical Velazquez is a portrait of a single figure, full length, standing with grave inconsequence in the quiet air of a shadowy, undefined room. *The Maids of Honor*, in spite of its complication and its anecdotal suggestion, has something of this mood.

Because we are so frequently told that Velazquez painted this picture as he saw the arrangement reflected in a large mirror, it is worth saying here that this idea is not as implausible as it may at first seem. If you will imagine yourself as the painter, standing before the easel and looking beyond at a mirror, you will see that it would be possible to arrange the figures in the room and paint them as reflected. You are facing your own reflection and looking at the reflected back of the tremendous canvas that will eventually be *The Maids of Honor*.

While Velazquez probably painted his own portrait from a mirrored reflection it is altogether possible that he did not paint the group as reflected and, even, that he never assembled all these people in the room at any one time. Yet the mirror idea gives a clue to the nature of Velazquez's realism: his art is a reflection of the world once removed through a medium that simplifies and intensifies our response to pure visual reality.

Jean Baptiste Siméon Chardin, 1699-1779, French

20. STILL LIFE: APPLES, PEARS, AND WHITE MUG

Oil on canvas. Height 13". Hon. and Mrs. W. Averell Harriman, New York

Chardin would have been surprised to hear his work described in terms of political philosophy as we have done here and probably as much surprised as gratified to discover how his reputation has increased in recent years. He was a quiet, simple Frenchman who led an uneventful middle-class life. He had a moderate but steady success throughout his life and was happy that circumstances allowed him to devote himself solely to his favorite subject, still life, during his last years. His paintings were admired and purchased for their verisimilitude to real objects. But Chardin's own pleasure was the problem of composition. He never tired of variations on his theme: a few simple objects harmoniously related as solid volumes in space. His preoccupation with the composition of forms was so fundamental to his concept of painting that in the twentieth century we think of him as a transitional figure between realism and contemporary abstraction.

Everything Chardin paints is recognizable for what it is. But these mugs, bowls, knives, pieces of fruit, and so on, are important to him first of all as forms. They are for Chardin only a point of departure just as they were in the next century for Cézanne when he made his revolutionary experiments in formal relationships. The difference, of course, is that Cézanne had no interest at all in sticking to the visual truth of the object. He distorted the objects at will for his compositions. Because Chardin represented objects so truthfully it is easy to accept his work at its semiphotographic face value and miss the underlying element of abstract formal organization entirely. But in the light of Cézanne's achievement Chardin's contribution is now revealed.

Jean Léon Gérôme, 1824-1904, French

21. THE DUEL AFTER THE MASQUERADE

Oil on canvas. Height 15¼". The Walters Art Gallery, Baltimore

Gérôme was one of the most successful artists painting in the academic tradition discussed in the Notes at the end of Portfolio 1. He cultivated a smooth surface adaptable to the sharp rendering of detail, an accomplishment that was all very well except that it was pointless. No exception can be taken to Gérôme technically: he is impeccable. The trouble is that his subjects are never vehicles for expression but only frameworks upon which to hang a demonstration of acquired skill. Typically, these subjects were exotic or high-flown ones borrowed and warmed over from painters who had given them meaning a generation or two before, but this meaning evaporates under Gérôme's parasitic treatment.

Our reproduction, *The Duel After the Masquerade*, is several cuts above Gérôme's usual achievement. The subject is less hackneyed; the contrast between the simplified background and the complicated figures is a departure from Gérôme's usual indiscriminately prolix detail; and finally the small size of the picture gives piquance to the miniature figures and modifies the pretentious air that is so stultifying in larger paintings of this kind.

Thomas Eakins, 1844-1916, American

22. MISS VAN BUREN, ABOUT 1891

Oil on canvas. Height 45". The Phillips Gallery, Washington

In the forty years since his death Eakins has steadily gained in recognition as a truly great and a truly American painter. He was born and raised and he worked and died in Philadelphia. For four years (1866–1870) he studied in Paris. Manet's *Picnic* and *Olympia* were still lively scandals. Yet Eakins was unaffected by the furor over the then modern artists as he was immune to the pedantry and pretension of those who attacked them. He had already studied at the Pennsylvania Academy of Fine Arts. In Paris he continued to take advantage of the best that his conservative teachers (one of whom was Jean Léon Gérôme) had to offer.

Returning to this country he managed to make a living by teaching and portrait painting. Since he never flattered a sitter he never became fashionable. Some of his portraits were refused and some others were accepted—and burned. Yet it is a mistake to think of Eakins as a neglected genius. He received some important commissions; we hear more about the people who resented his honesty than we do about those who recognized his merits.

In our recent self-conscious efforts to discover or synthesize an American spirit in painting Eakins's Americanism is conspicuous because it is genuine and spontaneous. There is about his art a soundness, a straightforward vigor, a rejection of artifice, a natural warmth, and a romantic perception of the mysterious and spiritual concealed within the ordinary. We like to think that these qualities are characteristically American.

Édouard Manet, 1832-1883, French

23. BOATING, 1874

Oil on canvas. Height 38¼". The Metropolitan Museum of Art

Manet was the best known and most vilified painter in France in 1863 and 1865 as the result of two paintings that caused the kind of furor possible in Paris alone, where the repercussions of an art exhibition may be not only intellectual but also social and political. In 1863 Manet's *The Picnic* (*Le Déjeuner sur l'herbe*) was the most scandalous painting in a scandalous exhibition, the famous Salon des Refusés, made up of paintings that had been rejected by the jury of the official Salon of that year. The scandalousness of the rejected pictures consisted of their originality and honesty, qualities that were naturally offensive to a jury dedicated to the cultivation of threadbare deceits.

The Picnic is now in the Louvre, along with Manet's *Olympia* of 1865, which caused an even greater scandal. The *Olympia* is a brilliantly executed portrait of a model named Victorine Meurend posed nude upon a couch. The picture is completely without the salacious overtones of the Salon nudes then in vogue, where flagrant eroticism was camouflaged by pretense of classical or symbolical treatment. Because the *Olympia* was an unidealized, matter-of-fact portrait of a young woman without clothes rather than a lascivious treatment of a female nude labeled "Venus," it was attacked as indecent.

Until the end of his life Manet was persecuted in the most reprehensible manner by critics and official painters. Their attacks usually invoked high and false moral values. Actually, the explanation for their venom is easy to see; it was frightening to the conventional established painters to see so original a talent, for in it they sensed their own doom. The great Zola was among the first critics to make Manet's cause his own. Others followed, and two years before his death the painter received a medal from an exceptional Salon jury, but the reward was too tardy to alleviate two decades of unreasonable hostility.

Manet was the oldest painter of the group later called the impressionists, of whom two, Degas and Renoir, were discussed in the preceding portfolio. Our reproduction, *Boating*, was painted fairly late in Manet's career when he was influenced by the impressionists' interest in effects of light and air outdoors.

Lascaux cave painting, Montignac, France

24. TWO BISON, BEFORE 15,000 B.C.

Mineral-oxide pigments on stone. Height 6'

The Cave of Lascaux near Montignac in France was discovered in 1940; a visit to it is as exciting an experience as the world of art has to offer. The very small original opening of the cave has been enlarged, and a minimum of changes has been made in the interior to permit illumination and more convenient observation; otherwise, the chambers look as they did some fifteen or thirty thousand years ago when the paintings were done. Of the various prehistoric paintings spotted around Europe, those of Lascaux and Altamira, in Spain, are the most numerous and the best preserved.

It is conjectured that the images were "painted" by rubbing natural oxides into the stone walls. Frequently the natural configuration of the wall is incorporated into the painted form, for instance, a bison's hump may be painted over a natural protrusion or depression of its approximate shape. The figures seem to be scattered over the walls without scheme; frequently new images were painted over older ones. Here and there the walls are obscured by an opaque limey coating from the secretion and evaporation of water, but for the most part the paintings have an amazing, vivid freshness.